The Truth About Suffering

The Truth About

SUFFERING

Why Does It Happen?

What Can We Do About It?

Steve Chalke
Paul Hansford

KINGSWAY PUBLICATIONS
EASTBOURNE

Scripture quotations taken from the HOLY BIBLE, NEW INTER-
NATIONAL READER'S VERSION. Copyright © 1994 by International Bible Society. Used by permission of Hodder & Stoughton
Ltd, a member of the Hodder Headline Plc Group. All rights
reserved.

Scripture taken from the HOLY BIBLE, NEW INTERNATIONAL
VERSION. Copyright © 1973, 1978, 1984 by International Bible
Society. Used by permission of Hodder & Stoughton Ltd. All rights
reserved.

Quotations from Elie Wiesel, *Night* (Penguin, London 1981), are
used by kind permission. Copyright © Les Editions de Minuit,
1958. English translation copyright © McGibbon & Kee, 1960. We
have been asked to make clear that Wiesel's comments represent a
Jewish, not a Christian, response to suffering.

ISBN 0-85476-634-0

KINGSWAY PUBLICATIONS LTD
Lottbridge Drove, Eastbourne, East Sussex BN23 6NT.
Printed in Great Britain by arrangement with
Bookprint Creative Services.
Designed & Typeset by Oasis Communications.

Contents

Part One
Why Does It Happen?

Part Two
What Can We Do About It?

Thanks to Nick and Erol
for their work on the text and cover.

God either wishes to take away evil, and is unable; or he is able and unwilling; or he is neither willing nor able; or he is both willing and able. If he is willing but unable, he is feeble, which is not in accordance with the character of God. If he is able and unwilling, he is envious, which is equally at variance with God. If he is neither willing nor able, he is both envious and feeble, and therefore not God. If he is both willing and able, which alone is suitable for God, from what source then are evils? Or why does he not remove them?

Attributed to the Greek Philosopher Epicurus.

INTRODUCTION

SUFFERING has long been a barrier to people believing in a loving God. 'After all,' they say, 'if God is so loving, and he knows about all this suffering, why doesn't he do something about it?'

This is a legitimate complaint. Like something from a courtroom drama, it puts God fairly and squarely in the dock, accused of negligence, impotence, or just a lack of compassion. For a loving and powerful God would never allow people to suffer as they do.

For centuries, Christians have argued in God's defence. They have used innumerable courtroom strategies to get God off the hook. They have denied the existence of the crime; they have claimed that suffering is 'good for the soul'; they have argued that good cannot exist without evil and suffering; or they have maintained that without the option to inflict suffering on others, people would not have the option of doing good.

And yet still, every day, the cry goes up all over the world: 'How can a loving God allow this to go on?' God may not have been convicted, but the jury is still out.

The main reason why Christians have largely failed in their defence of God is quite simply that they have not listened to their 'client'. They have often been so busy devising ways to prove God's innocence, that they have not realised him already entering a guilty plea for a crime he clearly has not committed.

What is more, he has been working to put matters right.

Yet rather than following God's example, Christians have frequently continued in their legal-style battle to clear his name. And in doing so, with all too few exceptions, they have failed to do the one thing that would demonstrate God's innocence beyond a shadow of doubt: act.

That's why this book has been written in the way it has.

I sincerely believe that it is we humans, not God, who should properly bear the blame for most of the evil and suffering in the world. And in Part One, I explain briefly why I think this is.

But it is not enough to stop there. For as long as we fail to do something positive to alleviate the suffering of others, we merely continue adding to it. A friend of mine was once asked to speak to a church group about world suffering. A few minutes before he got up to speak, the organiser checked with him what he was going to say. 'I'm not going to spend hours on the theory,' my friend said. 'I want to concentrate instead on what we should be doing about it.' 'Ah,' came the organiser's reply. 'So you're copping out, then!'

All too often, we're so wrapped up in the theory about why people suffer, being careful to dot all the 'i's and cross all the 't's, that we fail to do the obvious thing: take action. We need to act, just as God is acting, to make things better. In Part Two, I suggest a number of practical steps which you can take, both as an individual and as part of a wider group, to reduce the suffering which goes on around you.

I cannot emphasise strongly enough the importance of doing something more than just reading this book. As hackneyed as the phrase now sounds, it remains true: if you're not part of the solution, you're part of the problem.

As Martin Luther King said:

> *At the end of the twentieth century, most of us will not have to repent of the great evils we have done, but simply of the great apathy that stopped us from doing anything.*

Part One

Why Does It Happen?

Chapter One

THE JUGGLING ACT

Never shall I forget that night, the first night in camp, which has turned my life into one long night, seven times cursed and seven times sealed. Never shall I forget that smoke. Never shall I forget the little faces of the children, whose bodies I saw turned into wreaths of smoke beneath a silent blue sky.

Never shall I forget those flames which consumed my faith forever.

Never shall I forget that nocturnal silence which deprived me, for all eternity, of the desire to live. Never shall I forget those moments which murdered my God and my soul and turned my dreams to dust. Never shall I forget these things, even if I am condemned to live as long as God Himself. Never.

These are the words of Elie Wiesel, winner of the 1986 Nobel Peace Prize. They describe his reaction to his first night in the Nazi camp of Birkenau, 'reception centre' for the concentration camp at Auschwitz. Those who failed Birkenau's rudimentary 'selection' procedure, including his mother and his little sister, didn't even live long enough to make it to Auschwitz. With his own eyes, Wiesel saw children being thrown into ditches from which gigantic flames leapt up.

The fifteen year-old Wiesel, whose passion for God and love of Jewish teaching had been his whole life in his Hungarian town, saw his strong belief evaporate with those same flames. He had once spent his nights eagerly studying the writings of the Jewish mystics. But in the concentration camps, he found himself unable even to join in with prayers for the Jewish New Year.

> *This day I had ceased to plead. I was no longer capable of lamentation On the contrary, I felt very strong. I was the accuser, God the accused.... How I sympathized with Job! I did not deny God's existence, but I doubted his absolute justice.*

'Something's Got To Give'

Wiesel's complaint is a common one, although not everyone who voices it has been through so horrific an ordeal as a Nazi death camp.

The thinking behind it is very simple: the existence of suffering and evil in the world are incompatible with the

Jewish and Christian belief in an all-powerful and loving God. Surely if God cared about people who were suffering, he would do something to help. He would end their suffering. Yet people continue to suffer. Why doesn't God do something?

Perhaps God wants to do something, but can't. Perhaps ending the world's suffering is just too big a job. But in this case, God isn't all-powerful. Perhaps God is all powerful, but just doesn't care enough to end people's suffering. In this case, he isn't a loving God. Perhaps God does care and is all-powerful, but with his long-term view he doesn't see suffering and evil as real or as threatening as we do. Maybe they are actually all part of a huge learning process. In this case, suffering and evil are minimised, or even dismissed as being just an illusion.

For more than two thousand years, the majority of Christians and Jews have been trying to come to terms with a complicated juggling act. They have instinctively known that suffering and evil are not illusions. Yet they have firmly believed in an all-powerful God who loves his creation with every fibre of his being.

And like any juggling act, it has worked because one of these three factors - the existence of suffering, the all-powerfulness of God, and the overwhelming love of God - has always been up in the air. The juggler has rarely had to deal with more than two of them at any one time.

But like every juggling act, it needs real concentration to keep it going. And when all three balls come crashing down together, something's got to give.

Chapter Two

THE TRUTH, BUT NOT THE WHOLE TRUTH

A GREAT many Christians have 'solved' the juggler's problem of what to do when all three balls come crashing down at the same time by simply eliminating or ignoring one of the balls altogether. They have been unwilling to deny the love or all-powerfulness of God, which they quite rightly consider to be essential parts of the Christian faith. So they have resorted to using one or more of four different arguments which ignore or downplay the reality of suffering:

Suffering is really not all that bad.

Reports of terrible suffering and evil are either imagined or exaggerated. After all, that kind of thing just doesn't happen today.

Suffering and evil are merely small parts of a bigger picture.

In that context, suffering can actually prove to be a good thing, helping us learn and become more mature people.

Suffering is merely the result of people's own sin.

People reap the consequences of their actions. They have no one to blame but themselves.

Suffering is the inevitable consequence of a spiritual war.

So it isn't God who is responsible for the world's suffering, but the devil, and people who suffer are just the casualties of the war between good and evil.

There is, of course, a great deal of truth in these arguments. But although they do contain truth, none of them, either on their own or in combination with the others, contains the whole truth. They are pieces of a jigsaw puzzle, but not the whole picture. In this chapter, I examine the arguments one by one, and explain why they are not enough by themselves.

In a juggling act, ignoring one of the balls is a recipe for disaster. It's no good telling yourself that it doesn't exist, or that it's too lightweight to worry about. When it hits your toes, it still hurts! In fact, the shock can be so great that it causes you to drop the other two balls. Christians who downplay or ignore the reality of suffering are likely to end up losing their belief in the love and all-powerfulness of God.

1. 'Suffering is really not all that bad.'

In his account of his death camp experiences, *Night*, Wiesel records that his family and friends had numerous opportunities to avoid being deported to a concentration camp. Before the German troops arrived in their town, before the ghettoes were created, the night before they were loaded onto a train; at any time, they could have escaped and emigrated to safety in Palestine.

Yet they did not. They simply could not bring themselves to believe the stories told them of Nazi atrocities. Men being forced to dig their own graves, babies being tossed in the air and used for target practice. They dismissed these as rumours, lies or the tales of fools. It was unimaginable to them that people could behave this way in twentieth century Europe. Though they didn't deny the existence of suffering, their belief in an all-powerful God meant that they could not fully accept the scale or horror of its reality.

So when Wiesel was faced with an inhumanity more terrifying than he could ever have imagined, a form of suffering whose reality was beyond question, either the love or the power of God had to go. He could not bring himself to deny the existence of God, nor his power. So he came to doubt God's justice and love.

Others have faced a similar problem. Perhaps they have managed to juggle the reality of suffering with the power and the love of God for many years. But they have only been able to keep this going because they've never had to deal with the full impact of suffering at close quarters. For them, the problem of suffering has remained largely academic. The kind of suffering that makes people accuse God of being weak or cruel has happened to others, not to them. And this, of course, means that answers are easier to find.

Suffering comes at different levels of intensity and in different forms. If a person stubs their toe, they suffer pain. It is acute, but it doesn't make them doubt the existence or the love of God. But if their daughter is abducted, raped and killed, they may find themselves asking some pretty deep questions.

The exact amount of suffering needed to force a crisis of faith varies from person to person. There is no 'Universal Sufferometer' able to gauge the level past which a person will automatically begin to doubt God's existence or care. Some write off the idea of a loving and all-powerful God after watching pictures of famine on television, or when a friend is killed in a car accident. Others continue to believe in spite of having to go through the most terrible ordeals.

In the Old Testament, Job's faith survived the death of all his children and the loss of all his wealth on a single day. For most people, such a loss would have severely shaken any belief they had in divine justice. But Job's life and faith were extraordinary. In fact, it took a very painful and stigmatising skin disease, on top of all his previous suffering, before he questioned God's innate goodness.

It's only when we ourselves, or someone else very close to us, are afflicted by intense suffering that the 'answers' suddenly seem a lot more difficult to accept. This is simply because many of the 'answers', explaining why a loving and all-powerful God should allow people to suffer, depend on either lessening or denying the reality of suffering.

As a result, we are unprepared for the discovery that suffering and evil are, as Martin Luther King said, *'stark, grim, and colossally real.'* And that discovery, when it eventually comes, rocks our faith.

I will never forget my first trip to India. Although I had heard a lot about the country, which one critic has described as 'an assault on all the senses at once', nothing could have prepared me for what I encountered. The sheer scale of the suffering made me just want to run and hide. I didn't want to deal with what my eyes and ears (and nose) were telling me. And none of the explanations for suffering and evil I had been taught at theological college made any sense to me whatsoever in the slums of Bombay.

Denying or ignoring the colossal reality of suffering and evil are much easier to do, and much more common, than we would like to think. And as they say, 'ignorance is bliss'.

Martin Luther King is a hero of mine. He combined a firm belief in God with a strong belief in justice, and upheld the idea of God as loving and all-powerful in the midst of his struggle against one of the most destructive causes of suffering to have existed during my lifetime: racial segregation. Yet in his earlier years, he had doubted the full reality of this evil. In his most popular book, *Strength To Love*, King recalled the impact which nineteenth century liberal theology had on him during his final year in theological college. It taught that the world was getting better and better, and that suffering would soon be overcome by human ingenuity and technology. *'I was absolutely convinced,'* he wrote, *'of the natural goodness of man and the natural power of human reason.'*

In spite of his personal and painful experiences of racism during childhood, King downplayed the reality of suffering and evil because they didn't fit his theories. But before he reached the end of his studies, he had changed his mind. And he claimed it was only this which gave his faith the strength to survive the incredible suffering he saw and experienced during his involvement in the Civil Rights Movement, rather than being shattered at the first sign of real pain and cruelty.

2. 'Suffering and evil are merely small parts of a bigger picture.'

But imagining that suffering is less awful than it is, is not the only way in which Christians have denied its reality over the years.

Some people have argued that although suffering and evil are very real, they are merely small parts of a bigger picture. They seem awful only because they are so close, meaning that we can't get a true perspective on them. If we had the power of hindsight, these people argue, of seeing the bigger picture, then we would realise that suffering is like the darker squares in a patchwork quilt. They add colour. They add interest. Without them, everything would seem bland, dull and monotonous.

To proponents of this 'patchwork quilt' theory, times of suffering are short. And seen in the context of a person's life as a whole, they're nothing. What seems bad at the time will prove to be for the best in the long run. Instances of suffering can be seen as good if they are looked at from a different angle.

When a young man is crippled for life in a motorcycle accident, it seems like a tragedy. But when all his friends are later drafted and die in Vietnam, he realises that life in a wheelchair is better than no life at all, and his accident begins to seem fortunate.

When a couple's young daughter dies from leukaemia, it seems like a tragedy. But when it brings the rest of the family closer together, prompting them to resolve conflicts and hatred which have festered like a wound for many years, threatening to break the family apart completely, it begins to seem more positive.

A successful businessman is struck down with multiple sclerosis. But as a result, he learns to stop and smell the roses. He sorts through his priorities to discover what really matters in life. Two years later, his wife says that their marriage is stronger than it's ever been in the past.

A heavy smoker suffers a minor heart attack. The shock provides her with enough incentive finally to give up her nicotine habit and stop polluting her lungs.

A great many Christians, and Christian thinkers, have come to view suffering as being actually good for us in the bigger picture. It's a learning process. God inflicts suffering on people, or allows them to suffer, in order that they might grow from the experience. It's the pain caused by the prick of the needle used to innoculate against a lethal disease. It's the smack given a child to teach it not to play with fire. It's the voice telling us, 'Take your medicine: it tastes horrid, but it's good for you.'

These ways of looking at suffering are attractive. They solve the problem of juggling the power and love of God with the existence of suffering by arguing that suffering is not really all that bad. However painful it might seem at the time, seen from a different angle suffering can even be a good thing.

Of course, there is some truth to this. Martin Luther King said that 'unearned suffering is redemptive.' The author of Hebrews explains that suffering can be a discipline.

> *No discipline seems pleasant at the time, but painful. Later on, however, it produces a harvest of righteousness and peace for those who have been trained by it.*

> (Hebrews 12:11 NIV)

Many people who have undergone intense suffering would agree. They have grown as a result of their pain and suffering. They have learned valuable lessons from it. They have come to see the world in a new and more creative light.

Brian Keenan credits his four-and-a-half years in captivity in Beirut with having helped him to develop as a person. In a peverse way, he says, he is almost grateful to his captors for the lessons he learnt during his time as a hostage. Yet this doesn't mean that the immense pain and suffering he underwent from his captors was a good thing, or that he would do it all again if he got the chance!

I recently met a single mother who shares the same sentiments. She had her first child when she was just 15. By the time she was 27, she'd had three more by different absent fathers. She was forced to live on the edge of poverty, caring for her children as best she could in spite of poor housing and an uncertain future. She had learnt from her mistakes. They still hurt, but she was sure that they had made her a stronger, more mature person and a good mother.

It is the same with Easter. It is deeply ironic that we refer to the day on which Jesus died as 'Good Friday'. There was nothing good about it! The human race assassinating God incarnate is hardly a reason to celebrate. And the need for God to die as a result of the sin which we commit is no cause for glee. Good Friday can never be less than a tragic day.

But we know, of course, that it was followed by Easter Sunday. As Paul explains in his first letter to the Corinthians (15:17), if Christ had not risen from the dead on Easter Day, then our sin would have continued to hang around our necks like a lead weight, stifling God's gift of life, and our faith would have been useless.

The resurrection does not make the crucifixion anything less than a tragedy, but it certainly makes it more than a tragedy. Because tragedy is not the end of the story.

In the same way, we can learn from suffering and grow from it. But this doesn't make the suffering any the less. Nor does it make it any easier to live with at the time.

Whatever good can come from suffering in the long run is the result of God and human beings rescuing victory from the jaws of defeat. It doesn't make the suffering any less real. It doesn't make it any less wrong. It just stops it from being the end of the story. We must learn to be honest about this, instead of being glib or dismissive.

Suffering is a tragic thing. It doesn't seem to fit with the idea of an all-powerful and loving God. After all, many people suffer out of all reasonable proportion to the lessons they are able to learn from it. People can still suffer long after they have learnt how to appreciate life without suffering ... a life many no longer have the chance to appreciate!

And what about the times when no good at all seems to come from suffering? When there is no Happy Ever After? What if, rather than bringing their extended family closer together, as we suggested earlier, the death of a couple's daughter caused more division and hurt within the family? What if, unable to cope with the differences in how each came to terms with their loss, the couple grew apart, ending their marriage in divorce?

More to the point, perhaps, why could God not discover a way for people to learn these lessons without all the pain and suffering?

3. 'Suffering is merely the result of people's own sin.'

It is a very old belief that people get what's coming to them. 'As you sow, so shall you reap.' According to this theory, people's suffering is just the result of the sin they themselves have committed in their lives. God punishes people for the wrong they have done to him and to others. If they have caused other people to suffer, God will make them feel the effect of their actions.

This was the prevailing theory at the time of the book of Job. When Job's wealth is taken from him, his children are killed, and his body is covered in sores, he is visited by three friends. They are so shocked by what has happened to him that none of them speaks for a whole week. And when they do finally start talking, it's to tell Job (in as kind and gentle a way as they can) that he should repent of his sin! Then God will forgive him and restore to him his health and his fortune.

Job is outraged by his friends' suggestion. Whilst he does not deny that he has sinned, he knows that he has done nothing to warrant the kind of suffering he is now having to go through. Without his money, his family and the respect of his peers, all he has left is his faith and his innocence. His wife wants him to give up his faith, and his friends want him to give up his innocence!

People's treatment of Job convinces him that there's something wrong with the idea that people suffer for their sins. His friends remain firm: people *only* suffer for their sins, and since Job is suffering pretty badly, he must also have sinned pretty badly. In the end, when Job demands that they name his sins, they reel off a list of terrible crimes, many of which they have earlier specifically denied that Job has committed!

The reader, of course, knows something that Job and his companions do not. Having read the prologue to the book, they know that Job is suffering not because of his sins, but because of his lack of them!

As his friends become more and more convinced of his guilt, Job becomes more and more convinced of his innocence. He begins, like Elie Wiesel, to question God's justice. He knows that he is suffering unjustly, yet even Job can't quite shake off the belief that people suffer only for their sins. He cannot understand God's silence.

The breakthrough comes when he finally looks beyond himself and his own suffering to see the suffering of others. It occurs to him that, if he is suffering even though he is innocent, other innocent people must be suffering as well. And when he looks at the world from this perspective, everything begins to make sense. He comes to understand that it's not God's morality, or even his own morality, which is at fault. It's his theology. He finally breaks with the idea that people only suffer as punishment for their sins. He doesn't discover why people suffer - he leaves the exact reasons to God. But what he does know is that a lot of innocent people suffer because other people make them suffer!

Of course, people *do* suffer because of their sins. Not as a punishment perhaps, but as a consequence.

Picture this: in the middle of a beautiful but deserted beach is a sign saying, 'SHARK INFESTED WATERS: NO SWIMMING'. The sea is warm and inviting, and I ignore the advice and go swimming. I get eaten by a shark. My death is not a punishment for my stupidity, but the natural consequence of it.

In the same way, people often suffer the consequences of their own sins. After all, God doesn't call things sinful for nothing. Sin is destructive. In fact, in terms of a definition, something is a sin because it is damaging and destructive, not damaging and destructive because it is a sin.

But this is not the whole story. People can also suffer the consequences of other people's sins or mistakes. The children born to people with HIV, for instance, are clearly not to blame if they themselves are carriers of the virus, or subsequently contract AIDS, even if their father or mother got the virus by having casual sex. The idea that people suffer only for the sins they themselves have committed is wrong, and nowhere is this more clearly spelt out for the Christian than in the death of Jesus, who was totally without sin.

4. 'Suffering is the inevitable consequence of a spiritual war.'

Star Wars is a great film. Haircuts aside, it is an old-fashioned story of good triumphing over evil. Freedom triumphs over ruthless dictatorship. The puny David triumphs over a heavily armed and laser-toting Goliath. The good side of The Force triumphs over the dark side. It is an age old story in which the good guys struggle, but win in the end.

Throughout the history of the church, and for centuries before that, people have viewed suffering in the same way. Good will win out in the end, but people will suffer in the meantime as a result of evil people inspired by the devil. If people suffer from pain, disease or disablement, therefore, they are, in effect, the casualties of war - a war of the heavens, of good against evil, of God against the devil.

Sometimes, when the cause of suffering is mysterious, we resort to a kind of 'Devil of the Gaps' theory, just as many of our predecessors relied on a 'God of the Gaps' theory to explain what they didn't yet know about the world and how it functioned. Epilepsy, for instance, was once considered to have been a form of demonic possession.

It's obvious, even to the most shortsighted observer, that we are embroiled in a war between good and evil. And as in every war, whatever the outcome, there will inevitably be casualties. The allies won World War II, but this didn't stop men being killed or injured in campaigns such as the D-Day landings. African Americans won their battle to end legal segregation in the Southern states, but this didn't stop thousands of innocent men, women and children being beaten or killed in the process. Yet blaming things on the devil is often little more than a very convenient way of passing the buck.

Burnout amongst missionaries and church leaders runs at an alarmingly high level. They can be under enormous pressure, and the stress can sometimes prove to be too great.

When this happens, it's very tempting for us to blame the devil and chalk them up as casualties of 'spiritual warfare'. But under closer inspection, what often emerges is a picture of impossible demands being made with too little support and resources being given. The truth is, as long as we continue to pass the buck and blame the devil for our own mistakes, we will never learn from them.

Arthur Miller's play, *The Crucible*, is based on the true story of an infamous 'witchhunt' in the town of Salem, Massachusetts, in 1692. When a group of young girls began to scream, convulse and bark like dogs, three women were arrested for witchcraft, an offence punishable by death. They were brought before a special court. Accusations flew hard and fast, and many other women - and men - were also arrested. No one was acquitted. Those who 'confessed' were jailed, but those who protested their innocence were treated more severely. In the space of less than a year, twenty people were executed and two died in prison.

When the panic died down, however, many people began to express doubts about the safety of the convictions. The remaining suspects were acquitted. Historians now doubt the existence of any genuine witches in Salem at the time, pointing instead to factional rivalries among the townsfolk. Witches were just a convenient scapegoat, and the longer the people of Salem continued to blame them, the longer they were able to put off coming to terms with their own sins and inadequacies.

Miller wrote the play in 1953, the same year that Senator Joseph McCarthy's 'witchhunt' against supposed communists in the USA reached fever pitch. Almost everything that was wrong with 1950s America was being blamed on 'communist infiltrators', with the result that most normal Americans never examined their own hearts to look for the problems. Miller himself was investigated by the Senator's 'Un-American Activities Committee' three years later.

We can't simply blame the devil for everything that's wrong with the world and our own lives. Such a simplistic explanation of suffering and evil just doesn't fit the facts. Equally, we shouldn't go to the opposite end of the spectrum and dismiss the reality that

> *Our struggle is not against flesh and blood, but against the rulers, against the authorities, against the powers of this dark world and against the spiritual forces of evil in the heavenly realms.*
>
> (Ephesians 6:12 NIV)

As the saying goes, truth flies on two wings.

Chapter Three

ALL ABOARD
NOAH'S ARK

So if we can't ignore the reality of suffering, and we don't want to compromise on our belief in the love and all-powerfulness of God, what can we do?

'If God was so good and so powerful, he'd wipe out evil people,' some complain. 'Then there'd be no more suffering.' On the face of it, this seems quite a compelling argument. But the more deeply you look at it, the more this proposed `solution' introduces an even greater problem: exactly who are the evil people? After all, there's no internationally recognised scale for measuring a person's sins. So you can't determine who classifies as `evil', and who scrapes by because they are merely `bad', simply from reading off a chart.

In 1877, four years before his death, the great Russian novelist Fyodor Dostoevsky wrote a short story called *The Dream of A Ridiculous Man*. In it he attacked what he saw as false optimism about human nature. A man on the brink of suicide dreams of flying to another planet millions of miles away, identical to the Earth except that everyone there is innocent and happy. There is no sin or evil, and no suffering. The man is overawed by their beauty and their love.

> *But now,* [he recalls when his dream is over] *I will tell you the whole truth. The fact is, I - corrupted them all! ... Like the germ of the plague infecting whole kingdoms, so did I infect with myself all that happy earth that knew no sin before me. They learnt to lie, and they grew to appreciate the beauty of a lie. Oh, perhaps, it all began innocently, with a jest, with a desire to show off, with amorous play, and perhaps indeed only with a germ, but this germ made its way into their hearts and they liked it.*

In Dostoevsky's tale, the minor sins of one man were enough to corrupt an entire world, and over the course of thousands of years to make it just as bad as the one he had left.

The Bible tells a similar story: Noah's Ark (Genesis 6-9). Appalled by the amount and cruelty of people's sin, God instructs Noah, the only man he is prepared to call 'righteous', to build a boat, and to fill it with his family and a variety of animals. God will wipe the slate clean, destroying everyone else. Yet this fresh start is a false start, for no sooner has Noah got off the boat after the flood than he and his sons fall into sin.

Noah was a good man, yet even he was not upright enough to stop sin from creeping back into the world. And because sin is a corrupting influence, it only takes a small amount to do a lot of damage. So even if every truly 'evil' person were eradicated, we would soon find that things were as bad as ever. Because the only way to eliminate evil permanently this way would be to kill off the entire human race! As Paul told the Church in Rome, 'Everyone has sinned. No one measures up to God's glory' (Romans 3:23 NIRV).

Another writer, G. K. Chesterton, reflected this thinking in a letter to *The Times*. The newspaper had asked its readers, 'What's wrong with the world?' Over the course of a few months, all sorts of people wrote in suggesting answers. Chesterton's contribution was just two words long: 'I am.'

Suffering, in other words, is not merely caused by the Adolf Hitlers of the world. It can be caused by you and me: people who might consider themselves sinners, but would never agree to being called 'evil'. Ordinary people can cause immense suffering, even when they have the best of intentions. Sometimes it's a result of our doing bad things. At other times it's a result of our not doing good things. As the saying goes,

> *All that is required for evil to triumph is for good men to do nothing.*

Knocking The System

Some suffering, for instance, is caused not by malicious or sadistic individuals, but by unjust systems. If you've ever played the game Monopoly, you'll know what I mean.

When the game starts, all the players are equal. They start from a 'level playing field'. But this is not the whole story. In the opening stages of the game, the players are putting in place a system which will either work for them or against them later on.

You can really see this if, rather than playing the game to the end, players agree to swap positions once all the properties have been bought and houses or hotels begin to be acquired. Players who inherit poor hands find it much harder to stay in the game than those who inherit good ones. It takes extraordinary skill and judgement to recover if you own little property and no houses. By contrast, it takes almost no skill at all to win if you have inherited more hotels than anyone else.

In his bestselling book, *Savage Inequalities*, American educator Jonathan Kozol looks at the sharp differences in both funding and performance between public (state) sector schools in poor areas of the USA and those in rich ones. Annual spending per pupil can be as much as three times higher in rich districts than in poor districts, with the result that both academic performance and self-esteem are considerably better in the wealthy suburbs than they are in the deprived inner city.

Because of their better education and surroundings, the children of wealthy and successful parents stand a much greater chance of becoming wealthy and successful themselves than do the children of the inner city. Poor children are considerably more likely than well-off ones to turn to crime or take dead-end jobs, guaranteeing that their conditions won't improve.

Of course, no one ever made a deliberate 'policy decision' to exclude the children of the less well-off from a quality education. Over time, slight imbalances have simply become more and more exaggerated. Well educated parents have demanded, and got, a better standard of education for their children. Meanwhile, the children of poorer and less well educated parents, who usually lack the political clout and know-how to make the same demands, have lost out. The system of funding has slowly tipped in favour of the wealthier districts.

But just because this system was not set up deliberately by evil people, doesn't diminish the suffering it causes to the poor. Kozol warns:

> *It's not malevolent, the affluent suburbs do not wish the children of the poor ill. They simply want the most for their own children.*

The unconsciousness way in which an oppressive system can operate could be seen during the days of the apartheid regime in South Africa. Nobel Prize winner Beyers Naudé was brought up to believe that apartheid was the will of God. He even became a minister in the Dutch Reformed Church, but for a long time he never doubted what he'd been taught. He admitted later:

> *I never questioned this in any way critically, because I'd assumed that it was something that had been properly thought through.*

White people didn't need to hate black people in order to be supporters of apartheid. They simply needed to accept what society taught them. In fact, most whites considered apartheid to be a good thing for blacks. Apartheid was undoubtedly an evil system, but it wasn't necessary for white people to be actively evil in order for the system to continue to oppress black people. They just needed to be extremely misinformed and ignorant of the full reality of suffering which the system caused.

Writing to a friend from their Berlin bunker in the last days of World War II, Eva Braun expressed the same level of ignorance about the evil she and her partner, Adolf Hitler, had caused. *'I can't understand how all this can happen,'* she wrote, talking about the collapse of the Third Reich and the bombing of Germany's capital. *'It's enough to make one lose one's faith in God!'*

Of course, evil does not just occur on the level of systems. In our own time, we have seen the collapse of a nation which was living proof of this. Karl Marx believed that evil wasn't personal. He taught that people are basically good, and evil only exists within economic and political structures. So if you abolished capitalism, he argued, a system which gives power to the rich, and replaced it with communism, a system which gives power to the workers, you could eradicate evil and suffering in one move.

Because he believed that greed would die a natural death when capitalism was no more, Marx didn't build any checks and balances into his new system. As a result, when his ideas were put into practice in the old USSR, the ordinary people Marx wanted to help suffered immensely because their leaders were greedy, corrupt and evil.

Chapter Four

FREE WILL

SO WHERE does this leave us with the juggling act?

We have seen that suffering and evil are real, and that although good can eventually come from suffering, this isn't the whole story. It isn't just punishment for the sins we ourselves have committed, and it's not just the devil getting at us.

We have also seen that suffering isn't caused by just a few bad people. Good people can still cause suffering, even when this is the last thing they want to do: either impersonally through systems, or by doing the wrong thing and not doing the right thing. As Paul put it,

> *'I don't do the good things I want to do. I keep on doing the evil things I don't want to do'*
> (Romans 7:19 NIRV).

So for God to get rid of evil, he would have to get rid of every man, woman and child on the planet... and where would we be then?

We seem, therefore, to be stuck with the juggling ball of suffering. We can't ignore it, and we can't eliminate it. But, as Christians, we aren't prepared to compromise on our belief that God is both all-powerful and totally loving. So have we reached a dead-end?

Perhaps not. There is a way forward. It involves a closer examination of the two balls of love and power, and it's normally called the 'free will' argument.

Like many before him, Martin Luther King saw the apparent contradiction between God's love and power on the one hand, and the existence of suffering and evil on the other. As a human being, he couldn't, in all conscience, accept any explanation of suffering that downplayed its reality. He had seen far too much for this. But as a Christian, he couldn't see his way to accepting any explanation of God which downplayed his power or his love.

> *'I do not pretend,'* [he said] *'to understand all of the ways of God or his particular timetable for grappling with evil. Perhaps if God dealt with evil in the overbearing way that we wish, he would defeat his ultimate purpose. We are responsible human beings, not blind automatons; persons, not puppets.'*

How could a loving God create puppets, or 'blind automatons' like robots, when it was within his power to create people with the ability to love? For him to do this would be totally out of character, since he's a God of love. But in order to be able to love, people need to be able to choose.

42

And choice is freedom. As Elie Wiesel himself has commented since his ordeal:

> *'It was in order that we might be free that God chose to create us.'*

I love my wife. So every year, on her birthday and at Christmas, I spend ages racking my brains, trying to think of a present to give her that will express this fact clearly. I don't get her a present because I have to. I won't self-destruct if I don't. Instead I give it to her because I want to, because I choose to. And it's just because she knows that I have chosen to express my love in this way, that she regards the present as valuable. (Which is just as well, since it's rarely of value for any other reason!) However, if I gave her something simply because I was programmed to 'be nice' and had no choice about it, it would mean nothing.

Love cannot exist without choice. Because in order to be able truly to love someone, we first need the freedom not to love them; even to hate them, if we choose. Without this freedom, there would be no love, merely indifference, because we couldn't do things differently. Our behaviour would just be the result of the way we were programmed to perform. Freedom is the greatest gift that God could have given his creation, because it's the gift that truly brings us to life. To a God of love, a world of indifference   where there was no choice, no love, and therefore no real life - would be unthinkable.

43

'By endowing us with freedom,' [Martin Luther King continued, God] *'imposed certain restrictions upon himself. If his children are free, they must do his will by a voluntary choice. Therefore,'* [he concluded,] *'God cannot at the same time impose his will upon his children and also maintain his purpose for man.'*

When we discussed the juggling act at the beginning of this book, we looked at the nature of all three balls: God's love, his all-powerfulness, and the reality of suffering. We saw that many people have believed that if suffering is real, then either the all-powerfulness or the love of God have to go. The reason for this, it's claimed, is that if God really cared about people's suffering, he would do something about it. So the fact that he seems not to have done anything is a sign that he either doesn't care or can't do anything, contradicting either his love or his power.

The argument about our free will questions the basis of this. It takes a fresh look at God's all-powerfulness through the lens of his overwhelming love, arguing that it is precisely because he does care that he can't do anything about it. Because God loves us, he has given us a measure of power over ourselves and the rest of creation. And by giving it to us, God has limited his own use of it.

All this means that it's not so much that God's power is limited as *self-limited*. So the fact that God won't 'wipe out evil', far from being a sign of his weakness or lack of compassion, is actually a sign of his deep commitment to us and enormous care for us. He cares so much that he will not violate our freedom to choose. It's easy to end up with entirely the wrong idea about God's all-powerfulness and sovereignty. It's true that the Bible asserts that God is in control, but it's also clear that God has delegated power to the human race. His purposes will be achieved, but he has found a way of working them out without violating or manipulating our freedom to choose - our free will.

Of course, the problem with giving people a choice is that they are then capable of making the wrong one. And, as we all know, this is what human beings frequently do. As a result, the vast majority of suffering in the world is the inevitable consequence of humans making bad choices. And though they may not always make them deliberately, or with evil intent, they make them anyway.

With freedom comes responsibility. If we are free to make choices, then we must bear the blame when those choices turn out badly, and accept the consequences of our attitudes and actions.

In fact, we all understand this principle, and have made it a basic part of the way we function as a society. For instance, we limit the freedom children have to make choices until we think that they are wise enough to make good choices and old enough to take responsibility for them. We generally expect people to be held accountable for their actions, and our legal system reflects this idea.

Yet when it comes to God, many people want to have their cake and eat it. They want the freedom to behave as they choose, but none of the responsibility when this behaviour causes suffering and pain for themselves and others. The reality, actually, is that God would be responsible for the suffering we cause only if he programmed us to cause this suffering. But by giving us the freedom to choose our actions, God has also given us the responsibility for how we act. It cannot therefore be God's fault when we cause suffering through the choices we make.

Some people wonder whether God couldn't have done a better job designing people in the first place. 'Couldn't he have made people without moral defects, so that they would always make the right choice?', they ask. But this doesn't make any sense. People cannot be predetermined or designed so that they always make a particular choice; if they were predetermined, there would actually be no choice. And they would be robots, not people.

Back To The Drawing Board

But does this explain all suffering? Is it really that simple? Is it really true that human beings are the root of all the evils in the world by reason of their sin and their wrong choices? What about so-called 'natural disasters'? Tidal waves, hurricanes, typhoons, earthquakes, volcanic eruptions? Are we to blame for these as well?

The first thing to say is that no one actually considers hurricanes or earthquakes to be evil in themselves. A hurricane that destroys towns and families in a Caribbean island may prompt someone to lose their faith, but they're hardly likely to question the justice of God over a hurricane that comes nowhere near any form of civilisation. If anything, we are in awe of its destructive power. But no more and no less. Only when natural phenomena cause human suffering do we begin to look for someone to blame.

We are all aware nowadays of the brittle balance of nature, and the ways in which we have altered this balance. Whilst the jury is still out on issues such as global warming, it is already clear that ozone depletion and deforestation are major problems which will come back to haunt us, and that they are clearly human in their origin.

But we shouldn't think that it's a select group of masked and reckless eco-terrorists that maliciously have it in for the forests of the world. We all know that it's far more complex and system-wide than that. The fact is that economic priorities simply do not give seemingly irreplaceable forests and eco-systems a high enough value. Higher priorities, real or imagined, intervene. Valuable rainforest is cleared to allow the mining of precious metals, in the hope that this will bring revenue to an impoverished people. The poor chop down trees vital for enriching the soil in the long term, because they have no other means of fuel in the short term.

It may or may not be true that ill-thought-out environmental policies are adding to adverse weather conditions. It may or may not be true that the underground testing of nuclear weapons is damaging geological plates and increasing the risk of more earthquakes in test areas. What certainly is true is that human poverty is undermining the environment we are entrusted by God to steward, and is causing immense suffering. And human poverty is certainly not God's fault.

But even when, at first glance, it might seem that the cause of suffering has little or no link with the human race, and is quite beyond our control or responsibility, things are not always so straightforward. Take earthquakes, for instance. It is estimated that 1.4 million people have died this century as a result of earthquakes. Most of these deaths were caused by buildings collapsing and crushing their inhabitants. The technology to build 'earthquake-proof' houses and offices has existed for years. Most of the people who die in earthquakes, however, simply cannot afford this kind of housing.

As if to prove the point, when two earthquakes struck California in 1992, both measuring high on the Richter scale, they caused only one death between them. But the following year, another earthquake hit Maharashtra State, India. Although the shock didn't register very high on the Richter scale, more than 25,000 people lost their lives and 150,000 were made homeless in just 40 seconds!

Six months later, I visited this scene of devastation. In one village, I saw every house demolished except one, which had belonged to a rich man. In a village of homes built basically of stones, mud and wood, this was the only house to have been constructed from bricks and mortar on proper foundations. It didn't even have a crack in the plaster. Had all the houses in all 66 villages destroyed by the earthquake been built like this one, perhaps no one would have lost their life.

We may not be the cause of earthquakes, volcanoes or hurricanes, but we are certainly developing the technology to be able to predict much better when these things will strike, and to build cities which can withstand them. And of course, with the ability to do something about this kind of suffering goes the responsibility to do something about it.

Ironically, as our skills and understanding increase, and we feel more able to blame God for the apparent 'flaws' in his world design, so our ability to 'compensate' also becomes greater. The more we understand about the way our world works, the more informed our accusations against God become. But, if anything, they also become more irrelevant, because we ourselves become increasingly capable of limiting the amount of damage and suffering these 'natural disasters' cause, if we so choose. Whether or not we're in a position to blame God for doing nothing to alleviate people's suffering, we are certainly in a position to accept the blame ourselves for our own inactivity.

Even more ironically, our sense of outrage at the apparent injustices and the amount of suffering in the world only has any validity in the first place if we accept that it was created by a just and compassionate God. After all, if there is no God, there is no absolute right and wrong. If there is no ultimate source of authority, right and wrong are nothing more than personal, subjective views and opinions. Which, of course, means that any moral judgement about the state of the world is ultimately meaningless. Atheists may be able to view the suffering caused by natural disasters as tragic, but they can't see it as being in any way 'wrong' unless they consider humans to be totally at fault, because quite simply there's no one else to blame. It's just the way things have randomly turned out to be.

We may never know why God didn't make a world in which there were no 'natural disasters'. If we follow the thinking of the free will argument back to its logical roots, perhaps we could argue that God didn't just create human beings with freedom of choice, but all living things - right down to the atoms that make up the universe! And, as we've already seen, just as God isn't prepared to violate human freedom by stopping us causing suffering, so he's not prepared to violate the freedom of the rest of the universe.

Paul suggests that:

> *The creation was subjected to frustration, not by its*
> *own choice, but by the will of the one who subjected*
> *it, in hope that the creation itself will be liberated*
> *from its bondage to decay and brought into the glo*
> *rious freedom of the children of God*
>
> (Romans 8:20-21 NIV)

That's why the whole of creation has been *'groaning'* for the same hope that we have for the future, of a *'new heaven and new earth'* (Revelation 21:1).

God has created a world characterised by freedom and order, and he refuses to wipe out suffering in the way we'd like him to because this would involve him acting contrary to this freedom and order. And he will not do what is contrary to the laws of his universe and his own nature. If he did wipe out evil, as we want him to, we would find that it robbed us of everything we most value: the freedom that makes life life, and the order that makes the universe run.

Illness

A great many people find that their belief in the goodness and all-powerfulness of God comes to an end due to illness. And they don't even have to be the ones who are ill. In fact, more often than not, it's the friends and relatives of those who are ill who find illness such a problem for faith. And the more suffering an illness causes someone, the more likely it is to produce a crisis of faith for their loved ones.

Illnesses vary considerably in their intensity, and in the amount of suffering they cause. Winter sniffles aren't going to make anyone doubt the love of God, but it is rare for the parents of a child who develops leukaemia not to hold God at least partially responsible.

This is above all an emotional reaction, not a rational one. Of course, that doesn't make it any less real or any less valid. In fact, it is often because of the absence of any rational explanation that people come to view God as responsible for illness and disease. We can know that a disease is caused by a virus, but we're none the wiser as to why the virus exists in the first place. We can know that we all die in the end and that even a short life is better than none at all, but our instinct for life still sees a premature death as fundamentally unjust. And God seems to be the only one with the answers.

The Kenyan theologian John Mbiti records the reaction of many African peoples to the kind of suffering caused by illness:

> *'A bereaved mother whose child has died from malaria will not be satisfied with the scientific explanation that a mosquito carrying malaria parasites stung the child and caused it to suffer and die from malaria. She will wish to know why the mosquito stung her child and not somebody else's child.'*

Much like earthquakes and other 'natural disasters', the origins of disease frequently remain shrouded in mystery on the philosophical level. We simply don't know why disease exists any more than we know why earthquakes happen or hurricanes occur. We can trace their physical origin, of course, but we can't say why God created a universe in which AIDS and cancer can kill an innocent young child.

The free will argument offers the same insight into illness as it does into 'natural disasters': sin is possible even at the atomic level, and its consequences can be devastating. And God will not intervene if this means violating the freedom of the creation he loves.

But also much like 'natural disasters', the immediate reasons for much of the suffering that illness and disease cause can often be traced back to human beings. Bad sanitation, restricted access to basic medical facilities, inadequate health education, inadequate nutrition; all of these factors can multiply the possible effects of a disease. All are a result of the way in which we have chosen to structure our society and world. And all of them exist not merely in Third World nations, but in every major city in the world.

Disease can often be connected with lifestyle. For instance, stress is considered to be a major factor in increasing the body's vulnerability to various types of disease, including heart disease. A properly balanced diet is also important. Recent studies in Scotland have linked an increased risk of getting heart disease with people eating too much fried food.

Again, the fact that a person's chances of getting cancer are significantly increased if they smoke has been common knowledge for a long time, but we are now also becoming more aware of the effects of passive smoking. The tragic death of Roy Castle, one of Oasis' patrons, clearly demonstrated the risks. Roy was a non-smoker, and he considered it to have been his years of performing in smoke-filled rooms that were solely responsible for him contracting cancer. The truth is, we've only just begun to understand the impact that our lifestyle can have on our health.

And then, of course, the profit motive can play a crucial role. It's suspected that the risk of contracting Creutzfeldt-Jakob Disease, which attacks the central nervous system and causes dementia, is increased by eating beef infected with BSE. But in turn, BSE - or 'Mad Cow Disease', as it's otherwise known - is thought originally to have been caused by cattle eating contaminated feed, containing the ground-up brains of sheep infected with scrapie. And why are vegetarian cows being given sheep products in their feed? To pump them full of protein and make them more profitable in the marketplace.

When it was introduced into the European market in 1956, thalidomide was hailed as a wonder drug. In fact, its manufacturers specifically recommended the tranquiliser for use by pregnant women, because it was considered to be safer than its rivals. But by the time it was withdrawn from the UK market in 1961, there was a strong body of evidence that it was anything but safe. Thalidomide was blamed for causing abnormalities in the nervous system of adults, and an extreme form of stunted limbs known as phocomelia in babies whose mothers took the drug during a particular stage of pregnancy. It's estimated that as many as 10,000 babies were malformed as a result of their mothers taking thalidomide. And why were the dangers not discovered before it went on sale? Because extensive scientific testing takes a long time and costs a lot of money. In a hugely competitive market like the pharmaceutical industry, it doesn't pay to come second in the race to develop a new drug.

With advances in medical technology, of course, diseases which were once seen as terminal are now things of the past. Medical optimism has led us to consider it possible to cure any disease, given the time and money needed for research projects and medicines. But with this know-how goes a responsibility. Ironically, again, the very knowledge that allows us to accuse God of doing nothing about people's suffering, indicts us in turn for the same lack of action.

A Word Of Caution

We *should* ask the difficult questions about suffering. Faith in God is not an exuse to pickle our brains. We are rational people, with rational minds, in a rational universe which is open to investigation. And we are free to ask these questions because, rather than creating us as robots, God has given us this freedom.

But although there is a lot we can discover, the reality is that we don't have all the answers, and we never will. What's more, it would be arrogant to assume that we did have all the answers. Even God himself doesn't explain to Job why innocent people suffer; he merely verifies that they do contrary to the prevailing theology of Job's day. God refuses to allow his actions to be pigeonholed into a handful of simple explanations. He reserves the same freedom for himself that he has given to human beings. And if God doesn't answer all of Job's questions, we shouldn't think that it's our responsibility to answer them either - even if we could! So beware of cut-and-dried theology that reduces the whole world to manageable formulas and leaves no room for mystery.

God speaks to Job only at the very end of the book. The reason for this is not that God wants to make a dramatic entrance, but that he recognises Job's need to ask questions, as part of his grieving process. And so it is with other people's questions about God and suffering. Just like Job, many people who ask how God could allow suffering don't actually want answers. They simply need to ask the questions.

Telling a grieving mother that her child died because someone else abused the trust and power that God gave them isn't going to help. Her question isn't an analytical, technical or theological one: it's an emotional one. So it would be wrong to give an analytical, technical or theological answer. Hospital chaplains make it a policy *not* to provide answers, accompanying people instead through the grieving process as they ask the questions. In fact, people may well be able to answer the question themselves, and yet still feel the need to ask them. There really *are* no answers to these cries of desperation and grief, but it's important to allow someone to ask the questions, and to listen to them when they do.

In his foreword to Elie Wiesel's book, *Night*, the French novelist François Mauriac remembers the first time they met, when the young Wiesel interviewed him for an Israeli newspaper. Their conversation took a personal turn, and Wiesel recounted some of his wartime experiences. Mauriac describes his own reaction, the reaction that all of us should have in such situations:

> 'What did I say to him? Did I speak of that other
> Israeli, his brother, who may have resembled him -
> the Crucified, whose Cross has conquered the world?
> Did I affirm that the stumbling block to his faith

was the cornerstone of mine, and that the conformity between the Cross and the suffering of men was in my eyes the key to that impenetrable mystery whereon the faith of his childhood had perished? ... All is grace. If the Eternal is the Eternal, the last word for each one of us belongs to Him. That is what I should have told this Jewish child. But I could only embrace him, weeping.'

Chapter Five

THE BUCK STOPS HERE

THE problem with the juggling act has been resolved, to the best of anyone's ability.

It's clear from what the Bible tells us about a God who calls himself love that he limits his own power in order to give the creation he loves the freedom properly to live, choosing whether or not to love him back. Not only that, but the free will argument does justice to all three of the balls we feel compelled to juggle. We can reconcile our belief in a loving and all-powerful God with the full horror and reality of suffering, without having to compromise anything.

But if we stop here, assuming that we've somehow managed to get God off the hook, we actually miss the very heart of everything he himself chooses to say and do about suffering. All too often, Christians have defended God against accusations of weakness or cruelty simply by reciting what has become known as the 'free will defence'. In doing so, we have not listened to our client. Because whilst God could have explained this in painstaking detail to the prophet Isaiah, or written it on stone tablets to give to Moses, he chose a different approach instead.

Elie Wiesel remembers many prisoners being executed during his time in Nazi concentration camps, but none had more impact on him than the hanging of a young boy. Inmates were divided into camps, and this 'sad-eyed angel' had been a servant of one camp leader, who was trusted by the Germans. When he was found to have blown up the local power station, the leader was tortured and transferred to another camp. But the boy was also tortured, and then sentenced to hang alongside two adults. The rest of the inmates were forced to watch the execution, powerless to help.

As the three prisoners stood on the gallows, waiting to be executed, Wiesel heard a voice behind him ask, 'Where is God? Where is he?'

'Long live liberty!' the two adults cried out, in defiance of their execution. The child said nothing. The signal was given, and the three were hanged. The adults died instantly, but the boy was too light, and it took more than half an hour for him to die. During this time, all the other inmates were forced to march past and look at the executed men.

As he passed the boy, still barely alive, Wiesel heard the same voice behind him ask, 'Where is God now?'

You might have expected Wiesel, who had come to doubt God's love and justice, to have asked the same question.

Yet as he recalls,

> *'I heard a voice within me answer him: "Where is He? Here He is - He is hanging here on this gallows...."'*

What did Wiesel mean by this? Did he see in the face of the dying boy the *'man of sorrows'* who *'was oppressed and afflicted, yet he did not open his mouth'* (Isaiah 53:3, 7 NIV)? Was the death of this 'sad-eyed angel' a sign that God was suffering alongside him, or that God was equally helpless? Whatever Wiesel meant by his comment, no Christian can fail to appreciate its impact.

In looking at the issue of suffering, we have often been so concerned to get God off the hook, to defend him against unjust accusations, that we have not heard his own response to people's suffering.

We have presented our case in God's defence, and have sat down, content with our 'closing arguments', waiting for the verdict of the jury. What we have not realised is that, whilst we have been speaking so eloquently on his behalf, he has chosen to enter a plea of guilty to a crime we know he has not committed. We have been so busy explaining to people why God really can't do anything that we have failed to notice that in fact he *has* done something.

Though people blame God for doing nothing in the face of terrible human suffering, the truth is that he has actually been very active. If we haven't noticed it, it's because we've been looking in the wrong place.

When Jesus arrived in Jerusalem, he was hailed as a king and messiah by the crowds. But within one week the same crowds were calling for his head. Why? Mostly because Jesus had disappointed them. They had expected a War rior-King, and what they got was the Prince of Peace They had imagined that the Messiah would come in power and glory, and do away with the oppressive Roman army in one fell swoop. And when they found out that Jesus saw his role as Messiah in very different terms, they abandoned him.

As the American theologian Reinhold Niebuhr com mented:

> *One reason why his claims to Messianic authority*
> *were rejected by the leaders of the Jews was because*
> *they expected a Messiah who would combine per-*
> *fect power and perfect goodness.*

But their problem was that they did not properly un derstand the nature of `perfect power'.

Brian Keenan gives a good illustration of the different approaches to 'perfect power' when he talks about his cap tors in his book, *An Evil Cradling*:

> *For years we were chained to a wall or radiator, but*
> *they were chained to their guns; futile symbols of*
> *power, not power itself. This was something these*
> *men could never know: real power embraces; it can-*
> *not destroy.*

61

Jesus' approach to changing the world and ushering in the kingdom of God wasn't what people expected. It's still not what people expect, which is why they fail to understand what God is doing about suffering.

> *In his very nature, he was God. But he did not think that being equal with God was something he should hold on to. Instead, he made himself nothing. He took on the very nature of a servant. He was made in human form. He appeared as a human being. He came down to the lowest level. He obeyed God completely, even though it lead to his death. In fact, he died on a cross.*

(Philippians 2:6-8 NIRV)

Jesus didn't write a manual on '101 Answers to Tough Theological Questions'. He didn't come to explain suffering, or to defend God against the same accusations that we still hear today. He didn't show a way to avoid suffering. Instead, he came to suffer.

Jesus wept when his friend died. He felt pain when the soldiers whipped him. He got angry when he saw the moneychangers exploiting the people. He collapsed from exhaustion when he was forced to carry his cross to the place of his execution. He felt panic and stress in the garden of Gethesemane. He experienced the full range of human emotion, pain and suffering.

But as well as suffering himself, he displayed amazing compassion for other people, and constantly worked to do all he could to help whenever he saw them suffering.

The big question is: why did God choose to act in this way? And the answer is twofold: the first has to do with *his* character, and the second has to do *ours*.

Those who blame God for human suffering usually argue that it is inconsistent for a loving God to do nothing. And they're right But it's entirely consistent for a God who loves people unconditionally to take the rap for something he did not do, and to do this in a quiet and unspoken way. Jesus accepted his suffering and death willingly, because he knew he was accepting the blame not for his own shortcomings, but for the sins of the rest of humanity. And he knew that by accepting this responsibility, he would be saving us from having to face the eventual consequences of our actions ourselves.

Human beings are basically selfish. If the amount of suffering in the world is to come down, we will have to change. But the desire to change is more likely to come from the 'carrot' than the 'stick' Our own ability to love, and to choose right over wrong, is a response to the quality of love we receive, especially from God.

As John says:

> *What is love? It is not that we loved God. It is that he loved us and sent his Son to give his life to pay for our sins We love because he loved us first.*
>
> (1 John 4:10,19 NIRV)

As Reinhold Niebuhr said:

> *There can indeed be no repentance if love does not shine through the justice. It shines through whenever it becomes apparent that the executor of judgement suffers willingly, as guiltless sufferer, with the guilty victim of punishment.*

And that's just how God has chosen to act.
In the words of Dorothy L Sayers:

> *For whatever reason God chose to make man as he is - limited and suffering and subject to sorrows and death - he had the honesty and the courage to take his own medicine. Whatever game he is playing with his creation, he has kept his own rules and played fair.*

'Followers of the Way'

Jesus told his disciples,

> *Those who have faith in me will do what I've been doing. In fact, they will do even greater things.*
> (John 14:12 NIRV).

This has often been misquoted and misunderstood. What it actually means is that the church exists to carry on Jesus' work, but on a greater geographical scale. We can't possibly do more than him in terms of the nature of our care. He healed the sick and even raised the dead! But we can do what he did globally.

God loved the world so much that he did something to end people's suffering and offer them a 'full' life (John 10:10): he sent his son to die on the cross. Sitting in comfortable chairs on carpeted floors, the modern church instead plans a leafleting campaign. When God said he loved the world, it cost Jesus his life. When we say we love the world, we should expect it to cost us the same.

This means that the church exists to continue God's way of ending suffering. It also means that Christians shouldn't expect their days of suffering to end the moment they become Christians. Because in the end, the way in which Jesus alleviated people's suffering was by taking it on himself.

The first Christians expected suffering. It was all par for the course. It was not simply that Christianity became an illegal religion within the Roman Empire. It was more deeply rooted than that. Jesus had demonstrated that love was about responding compassionately to people's needs, even when this meant being self-sacrificial. His followers understood that by living their lives with the same kind of love, they were opening themselves up to the same kind of fate, especially when this strong kind of love required exposing and confronting people's vested interests. So what was important to them was not living a pain-free life, but living self-sacrificially to relieve the pain of others.

As one critic of Evangelical Christianity has stated:

"The world has no problem believing in a poor carpenter's son who gave his life for others. What it cannot stomach are rich preachers who get fat telling the world about a poor carpenter's son who gave his life for others."

This is one of the reasons why the New Testament writers didn't seem to consider pain and suffering to be such terrible ordeals for the Christian.

Dear friends, don't be surprised by the painful suffering you're going through. Don't feel as if something strange were happening to you. Be joyful that you are taking part in Christ's sufferings."

(1 Peter 4:12,13 NIRV)

At times, the New Testament Christians took strength and comfort from their suffering, because it seemed to prove that their faith was genuine, and that they were living their lives as Jesus had lived his. And, of course, they knew that they weren't suffering alone. They knew that Jesus was with them through their suffering, *'through the valley of the shadow of death'* (Psalm 23:4 NIV).

Christians are not therefore immune from suffering. Becoming a Christian doesn't mean that your suffering has come to an end. In fact, it can often mean exactly the opposite. By becoming a Christian you open yourself up to

66

all kinds of suffering. It's the direct result of a lifestyle choice that puts the welfare of other people ahead of your own welfare. And it isn't masochistic - Christians don't choose the path of suffering because they like it. They choose it because their love for other people means that they are prepared to suffer themselves in order to alleviate the suffering of others. So Christians don't actually *choose* to suffer. They choose a way of life that sometimes involves suffering as a by-product.

We have already seen that, whilst suffering can never be a good thing in itself, good can come out of it. In fact, Jesus told his disciples to think of suffering as pruning, during which God *'trims every branch that does produce fruit. Then it will produce even more fruit'* (John 15:2 NIRV). Peter advised his readers to think that, *'your troubles have come in order to prove that your faith is real'* (1 Peter 1:7 NIRV). And Paul told the church in Rome,

> *We are full of joy even when we suffer. We know that our suffering gives us the strength to go on. The strength to go on produces character. Character produces hope. And hope will never let us down.*
>
> (Romans 5:3-5 NIRV).

So if we are 'followers of the Way', as Christians used to be called, we should be working to end other people's suffering just as Jesus did (and still does), even when this means increasing our own. And it's when we do this that others will be able to look and see that, through us, God is *still* doing something about the problem.

Jesus responded to people's suffering in a number of different ways When some of John the Baptist's disciples came to Jesus to ask him, *'Are you the one who was to come, or should we expect someone else?'*, Jesus replied:

> *Go back to John. Report to him what you hear and see. Blind people receive sight. Disabled people walk. Those who have skin diseases are healed. Deaf people hear. Dead people are raised to life. And the good news is preached to those who are poor.*
> (Matthew 11:4-5; cf Luke 4:18-19 NIRV)

Jesus considered these things to be the 'proof' that he was who he said he was. As his followers, we need to give the same kind of proof that he is who we say he is. So it's not enough simply to trot out well articulated arguments about 'free will' Instead, we need to work hard to eradicate people's suffering.

At times, God chooses to intervene and end suffering or pain miraculously. But his Spirit isn't just present in what we have too narrowly defined as 'the miraculous'. The Holy Spirit is equally at work in medicine and social care, and every action undertaken in Jesus' name.

In all this we must pray without ceasing and recognise our total dependence on God's strength and guidance. But we must never fall into the trap of regarding prayer and dependence as alternatives to action. They are simply the fuel to keep our action going.·

Part Two

WHAT CAN WE DO ABOUT IT?

Chapter Six

The Task Ahead

THERE IS, of course, no great single thing to be done about the great universal problem of suffering. There's no magic button to press that will instantly cure the world of all its problems and end suffering tomorrow. If there were, God would have pressed it long ago. So we should not expect the task ahead to be easy. Forget the cape and underpants, saving the world is a slow and laborious process.

Mother Teresa was once asked how she intended to feed all the hungry children who came to her in Calcutta. Her reply was sobering: 'One at a time.' She didn't see a huge 'problem'; all she saw was individual people in need. And she planned to respond to their need, one at a time.

It's very easy for us to become daunted, and then crippled, by the overwhelming level of suffering we see in the world around us. It can become like a crushing weight. We get to the point where we are convinced that the problem is so big, and we are so small, that there is no way we can ever make a real difference. But to see things this way is to see them from the wrong perspective. It is to see the huge 'problem', not the individual people or the possibilities to take action.

The Incarnational Approach

When God decided to 'intervene' in human affairs, to save the world, he did so as a human being. And not as a fore-runner of Superman, the invincible 'man of steel', but as a real human being, with ordinary needs, desires and weaknesses. In fact, although he healed people and performed extraordinary miracles, the most astonishing thing about Jesus was not his divinity at all, but his humanity. He coped with the same hunger, anguish, and even fears, that we do.

Jesus didn't publish a landmark 'Report On Suffering' spelling out detailed procedures to be followed in order to eliminate it all. He didn't found a great Institute or Academy to continue his philosophy. And he didn't start a political party to change the world, although many expected this of him. What he did do was respond to people: their needs, their fears, their hopes, their dreams. And he expected his followers to do the same.

So for us, instead of ending up paralysed by the enormous scale and complexity of suffering in the world around us, our task is to target and concentrate on what we can realistically do, instead of doing nothing. Jesus had a world plan and a strategy, but it started with responding to people around him and their needs, as these arose.

And in all of this, he always treated the people he encountered as whole people, never just as victims of various kinds of suffering. So, for instance, when he encoutered a person who was paralysed (Matthew 9:1-8), whose friends had brought him on a stretcher, Jesus did not immediately tell him to get up and walk. He knew instinctively that the man's problems were bigger and more complex than simply being unable to walk. In those days, many people believed that all who suffered physically in one way or another were paying the price for their own sins, or even for the sins of their parents (cf. John 9:2). No doubt the man also believed that he was paralysed because of sin. Jesus recognised that he needed more than the ability to walk. So he told him, 'Your sins are forgiven.' And the man walked In the same way, we should never treat people who are suffering as merely victims, but as whole people.

People are complex. Their suffering rarely has just one cause, and they understand and deal with it in different ways. Recognising this, the caring profession has changed many of its terms in the last few years. For example, labels such as 'the disabled', 'the blind' and 'the deaf' were used until quite recently. But attempting to emphasise the humanity, rather than the victim status, of people with reduced mobility, vision or hearing, they are now usually refered to as 'disabled people', 'blind people', 'deaf people'. In the same way, what used to be known as 'mental handicap' is now called 'learning difficulty', and many charities have gone as far as changing their names. (The Spastics Society, for example, is now known as Scope).

In all this, the aim is to stop thinking of people one-dimensionally as 'victims', and to emphasise their status as whole people - to put people's suffering in the context of the rest of their lives.

A Sub-Christian Occupation?

One of the problems which has dogged and damaged the Evangelical church throughout this century has been the dominant view that 'social work' either detracts from or adds to (depending on your perspective) the 'real' task of preaching the gospel.

Some Christians have suffered from a sort of 'Second Coming paralysis', in which the urgency of giving everyone the chance to become a Christian before Jesus' return has effectively put an end to all other activity. 'It's all very well to get involved in social work,' they argue, 'but what's really important is getting them saved. We should leave the rest to the social workers.'

Others see social action as something that complements the essential work of evangelism. According to the popular image, the gospel is not a sword but a pair of scissors, with twin cutting edges: evangelism and social action. The evangelism blade is very sharp and capable of cutting on its own, but using the second blade as well can still prove to be of great value.

But however eloquently they are illustrated, both of these views are wrong. Social action is actually an evangelistic task and responsibility. It's part and parcel of preaching the gospel. When Jesus began his ministry, he set out what he was going to do in a kind of manifesto or job description, taken from the book of Isaiah:

> *The Spirit of the Lord is on me, because he has anointed me to preach good news to the poor. He has sent me to proclaim freedom for the prisoners and recovery of sight for the blind, to release the op-pressed, to proclaim the year of the Lord's favour.*
>
> (Luke 4:18-19 NIV)

Over the years, Christians have often been guilty of making one of two great mistakes with this passage.

1. We have 'spiritualised' its message.

'You see,' we tell ourselves, 'when he says "poor", Jesus doesn't literally mean "poor". He means "poor in spirit". He's referring to all those who don't know him as their personal Lord and Saviour.' But in terms of the Hebrew thinking that Jesus grew up with, this kind of false division between body and spirit just didn't exist. People didn't think that way.

In fact, rather than coming from the Old Testament, or even from Jesus himself, this tendency of compartmentalising and 'spiritualising' things belongs to pagan Greek philosophy! As a Jew, Jesus would have thought quite differently - holistically. By 'poor', he would have meant those impoverished by any kind of hardship in any area of life: spiritual, social, political, emotional, physical, psychological, educational, financial, etc.

2. We have devalued its message.

The second mistake is to think of the message of most of this passage as being somehow secondary to the 'real' gospel. 'Of course we should help the poor, free prisoners, and release the oppressed,' we argue, 'but we do these things because of the love and compassion we have as Christians. They are consequences of the gospel, not part of the gospel itself.' But this popular view is also dangerously sub-Christian.

The truth is that our word 'evangelism' literally means to 'preach good news', and is the word used in this passage. Jesus is stating here that he sees his mission in terms of 'evangelising' the poor. And what is clear both from the rest of this passage, and subsequently from his life, is that 'evangelising' the poor is never just about preaching at them. It's about meeting their needs as whole people.

Good evangelism is a healthy tension - a tension that Christians are often guilty of getting wrong. Either we become almost apologetic about our faith, assuming that no one will really be interested in beginning a relationship with Jesus, or we end up almost ignoring people's other needs, spending all our effort on shoving our message down their throat whether they want it or not. And whilst 'liberal' Christians frequently make the first mistake, 'Evangelicals' often make the second.

By contrast, Jesus was sensitive to people's needs and wants, and responded to them in an appropriate way. He healed people who needed healing, forgave people who needed forgiveness, inspired people who needed vision, taught people who needed direction, dined with people who needed friendship, challenged people who needed discomfort, encouraged people who needed self-confidence, affirmed people who needed self-esteem, and offered a new life to those who were prepared to accept it. Rather than treating people as mere targets for conversion, Jesus treated them as whole people, reacting to their needs and working with them to end their suffering.

We need to understand our own role in exactly the same way. It is obviously true that, at heart, everyone needs to be 'born again', as Jesus himself expressed it to Nicodemus. But we will find it extremely difficult to introduce people to a relationship with Jesus if they 'smell a rat', and suspect that our concern for them starts and ends with their 'spiritual' health!

It's vital that we never think of work aimed at alleviating people's suffering as a kind of foreplay to the 'real' task of evangelism. If you're planning to set up a hostel, for instance, or a financial advice centre, don't be tempted to see it as a complicated device by which you might eventually earn the right to tell its users about Jesus. On the other hand, if your clients ask you why you set up the project, don't be shy in telling them your motivations as a disciple of Jesus. (Hopefully, however, they will already have seen much of this through the quality of your attitudes, behaviour and care.) Respond to people's needs as they arise. If they ask about money, tell them about money. If they ask about Jesus, tell them about Jesus.

Chapter Seven

PREPARING FOR ACTION

So IF IT's our God-given responsibility to take action, and relieve suffering whenever we encounter it, how should we go about doing this? There are basically two ways in which we both can, and should, respond.

1. Reactively, on a one-to-one, personal level. We don't need to go out looking for opportunities for this kind of care and action, because they will naturally come our way every day. We all know and meet people who are suffering in one way or another, and Jesus spelt out clearly our responsibility to help them in his parable of the Good Samaritan (Luke 10:25-37). It's clear that he had no time for the busy religious people he described who, because of other, bigger commitments and responsibilities, felt able to walk by and ignore the suffering of the individual they encountered.

2. Pro-actively, asking questions about the needs and suffering that exist within our communities and on a wider scale. This involves thinking through how to equip ourselves to meet people's needs as individuals, as part of a larger group, or as a church. Jesus himself travelled beyond his home town to help those in need, and told his followers actively to go, becoming his witnesses 'in Jerusalem, and in all Judea and Samaria, and to the ends of the earth'(Acts 1:8 NIV).

Since reactive help doesn't need advance planning or strategy, the rest of this book concentrates on things you can do pro-actively to help alleviate suffering. A few examples of the kind of thing you can do are outlined in the next chapter. But before you begin anything, it's important to take stock of both your opportunities and your resources. It's vital that you don't just get carried away, either by your enthusiasm or your compassion. You should also be careful to match the real needs of your local area - or wherever it is that you plan to help - with your resources.

> *Suppose someone wants to build a tower,* [Jesus warned.] *Won't he sit down first and work out how much it will cost? Then he will see whether he has enough money to finish it Suppose he starts building and is not able to finish. Then everyone who sees what he has done will laugh at him. They will say, 'this fellow started to build. But he wasn't able to finish.'*

(Luke 14:28 NIRV).

Know Your Community

It's vital, as you start thinking about any kind of planned involvement, that you take the time to carry out thorough research into the real needs that exist before you take action. This is especially true if it's a project which will include the use of other people's time, money, skills and resources. Here we are going to focus on how to assess people's needs in your local community, although the same principles apply in a different way to any type of social action projects you undertake anywhere in the world.

It's impossible to overemphasise the need to ensure that your ideas match the community's needs. For example, it's pointless opening a hostel for homeless young people if the pressing need in your area is for adequate short-term housing for homeless families. Similarly, there's little point sinking all your money and time into buying a specially adapted minibus for transporting physically disabled people, if all the disabled people you are in contact with already have cars, or if what they really need is full disabled access to your centre and its facilities.

Christians are often much better at talking than listening. All too often the result is that, rather than responding to the needs people actually have, we fall into the trap of responding to needs we think they have, or should have.

You obviously want to assess the strengths, weaknesses and needs in your local area before you start planning any grand schemes. Here are four steps to discovering the needs of your local community.

1. Discover its demographic mix

Who lives there, what is their age, gender, race, class, work, etc? This kind of statistical information can be found from your local library or town hall.

2. Discover what's already happening.

Find out about the groups, organisations and activities that already exist in the area. Lists of most of these can be found in your library, Thompson's Directory, Council offices or the local Citizens' Advice Bureau.

Don't duplicate unnecessarily: only set up a project to meet a real need that isn't being met or adequately catered for. So if there are already fifteen soup kitchens, and your area is awash with rivers of soup on a Friday night, don't make it sixteen!

3. Discover the real needs.

Talk to the various statutory authorities and voluntary agencies that already work with local people in different fields. The great mistake that many overseas Aid and Development agencies made in their early days was to start projects they thought were important, but which just didn't fit with the needs and desires of local populations. You'd be surprised how easy this mistake is to make, even when you're deliberately trying to avoid making it. So listen very carefully to what people tell you about their needs before you take action.

4. Discover what people think.

It's now time to make your own assessment of the needs of your local area, checking to what extent the experts' opinions match up with what 'the people' think. Conduct a survey, either door-to-door or perhaps in your local shopping centre. You'll have to think about and compile this carefully, in order to guarantee that it will eventually provide you with the information you're looking for.

Preparing a Survey

A sample questionnaire is contained at the back of this book, but don't just copy it word-for-word. Make sure you adapt it carefully to suit your needs and your community before using it. Without adequate planning and thought, it's surprisingly easy to find that you've made the mistake of asking questions that don't actually give you the information you most need. So rather than rushing into something prematurely, take the time to think through and plan your questionnaire carefully.

As you do, bear in mind the following points:

• Keep it short.

Questions should be brief and to the point, and arranged so that they flow as naturally as possible.

• Use tick boxes.

Use boxes rather than open-ended questions, wherever possible. This will make it much easier for you to gather statistics from your research, especially if you're using a computer to help you.

• Suggest possible areas of concern.

This will help focus your interviewees' thinking. But be careful never to be so rigid that people don't feel free to point out needs you've not listed. If you do, you won't find out what other people think - only what you already thought.

• Word questions carefully.

Avoid ambiguity. If your interviewees are unclear what they're being asked, you won't learn much from their answers.

• Don't ask unnecessary questions.

If you're not absolutely sure what information a question will give you, and what value it will be to you, don't ask it!

• Make it look professional.

Print your survey form on white A4 paper. Don't be afraid of white space - if your form looks amateur, it won't be taken seriously. It should state clearly at the top what it's for and who you are. Make sure it carries your church's logo.

• Road-test it.

Do a small test run (10-20 forms) with the public before you carry out your main survey. This will give you the chance to weed out any last minute problems and fine-tune your form

Using a Questionnaire

House-to-house visiting is fraught with difficulties, and isn't made any easier by the fact that some churches have in the past used bogus 'questionnaires' as a pretext for getting people to talk about the gospel. Needless to say, this is not your aim You genuinely need the information that a questionnaire can give you. And although you should never refuse to talk about your faith if people ask you, it must be clear both in your own mind and in the minds of the people you survey why you are there.

Approach one of your local papers ahead of time to get them to publish the results of the finished survey. You can then explain that this will be happening to those who take part. If possible, give them the date when the results will appear.

Before you conduct your survey, remember:

• Rehearse your interviewing team's fluency and technique Make sure they understand why each question is there and how long the whole form will take to answer. Use members of your church as 'guinea pigs' for them to practise on

• Inform the local police that you'll be conducting a survey, telling them where, when and why you'll be doing it. Ensure that they have no objections before you start. Especially if you're conducting your survey door-to-door, informing the police beforehand could save you some embarrassment later on.

• Decide whether you're going to survey people on their doorsteps, at the local shopping centre, or in some other location.

• Get your 'sample' size right. If the number of people who complete your survey is too small, it will reflect individual views rather than shared opinions. It therefore won't be accurate. But if you interview too many people, all you'll succeed in doing is wearing out your interviewers without discovering anything new. Make your survey no smaller than 100 and no bigger than 500 completed questionnaires.

• Make sure your sample is representative of your community. It's important that you cover the breadth of age, race, gender, social background, etc, that make up your 'patch'. Once again, this is essential if the understanding of local needs that arises from your survey is to be accurate. If the potential need you are thinking of tackling is contained within just one section of your local community, then your goal should be to survey a representative sample of that particular group.

When you conduct your survey, remember:

• Always carry identification. Give each interviewer an official-looking, laminated badge. Put on each badge the interviewer's name, their photograph, and your church's logo and telephone number. If your church has a printed T-shirt or sweat shirt, encourage each interviewer wear one.

• When you knock on someone's door, or stop them in the street, many will - quite understandably - be reluctant to talk. So begin by asking potential interviewees if they would be prepared to take part in a Community Survey. Make sure they can see the survey form and your identification. Tell them your name, and briefly explain who you are and why you're doing the survey. Give them a clear idea of how long it will take.

• If someone you approach declines to take part, respect their decision, thank them and move on.

• When people agree to complete your survey, always start at the beginning and work your way systematically through it, completing all the questions. Let them see the questions as you ask them, and their answers as you write them down.

• When you've completed all the questions, thank your interviewee for their time, remind them of when you expect the results to appear in the local paper, and move on.

Know Your Church

Once you have determined the needs and character of your local community, you are in a much better position to determine how best to respond as a church. Make the information you have collated available to your entire church membership. Discuss whatever projects you come up with openly, listening hard to the whole church and their insights. It's very shortsighted to plunge into an initiative which will require considerable resources without adequate support.

Above all, keep three things in mind:

1. Match the needs of the community with the skills and resources within your church, or group of churches.

Part of working out what you *should* do to help alleviate the suffering you see around you is working out what you *can* do. You may find that you lack the necessary skills, staff, budget or resources to respond to what your survey, and other research, has highlighted as the primary need in your area. But you are able to do something about a secondary cause of concern.

2. Never bite off more than you can chew.

In each of the example projects suggested in the next chapter, there are three levels of commitment: low, medium and high. Make a careful assessment of the amount of time, resources and personnel you can realistically commit to this area of ministry. You won't be doing anyone any favours by starting something you can't finish.

3. Never let the project itself overwhelm the people involved.

There will inevitably be mountains to climb in terms of organisation, fundraising and management - especially if you opt for a project which requires a high level of commitment. But never let the bureaucracy take over. If you do, your team of helpers will eventually lose both their trust and their interest in the project. Even worse, the very people whose suffering you are trying to lessen will end up feeling like victims and objects, not capable human beings.

Taking On The System

Once you become involved in a project to help meet the needs of your local community, you will discover that you are on a learning curve - not only about the particular issue you are tackling, but about all sorts of related ones as well. You will also soon discover the limits of your particular project or scheme. But don't let this put you off. Remember, you can't expect to end all suffering entirely on your own.

As we saw in Part One, suffering can be caused by personal factors or by evils within a system. But it's more usually a combination of both. So, especially if you're setting up a high commitment project, you will inevitably find

91

yourself becoming involved, to a greater or lesser extent, in the wider, political aspects of that issue. Don't be afraid of this: it's all part of bringing 'good news'.

The more you get involved with any particular issue, the more you will see past the symptoms you have to tackle initially, to the roots of the problem involved. These are usually as much to do with systems as personal circumstances, and you will need to tackle them at the same time as offering help to the victims of the problem.

Involvement at personal and political levels are not alternatives. In fact, when political solutions fail, it is often because the people who proposed them didn't listen well enough to those involved in a practical way on a personal level. And practical projects, essential as they are, nevertheless have their limits.

Christians have often been very wary of political involvement. Somewhere along the way, many of us have picked up the idea that 'politics and religion don't mix'. But as Archbishop Desmond Tutu said:

> *When people tell me that politics and Christianity do not mix, I wonder which Bible they have been reading.*

It is the responsibility of both individual Christians and the church to opt in, not opt out, politically.

In his book, *The Soul of Politics*, Jim Wallis writes:

Politics is the discourse of our public life There are real limits to what politics can provide to better the human condition. But politics can make a great difference, for good or evil, in the ways that we live together.

Chapter Eight

LEVELS OF COMMITMENT

THE FOLLOWING pages contain examples of some of the things that you and your church could do to help alleviate suffering in your community and further afield. But they are only examples, so don't tie yourself down to them. Instead, use your imagination in order to design other practical responses you can make.

For each area, I've broadly categorised three levels of commitment, so that you can work out what's right for you:

• **Low.**

This description categorises action on the part of individuals, or churches which are constrained by other commitments or a lack of resources. They all involve working in or alongside existing projects.

• Medium.

This category involves taking the initiative to set up a new project yourself. You'll therefore need the backing of a dedicated team. Any project in this category will require a substantial investment of time and money.

• High.

These projects all involve taking a significant risk. You will need to work in partnership with existing voluntary agencies, statutory authorities and other local churches to set them up, for which you will need an open mind and a flexible approach.

1. Debt

Debt is an extremely widespread problem which affects a huge number of people for a varietyof different reasons, many of them totally unforeseeable. Its impact both on the 'victim' and those around can be enormous. Financial worries can lead to depression, illness and eating disorders, as well as addictions, including smoking, gambling, heavy drinking, drugs, shoplifting and even compulsive spending! And *Relate* say that finance is cited as a major factor in marriage breakdown by over 70% of the couples they counsel. But strange as it may seem, debt isn't a problem which can be solved simply - or even primarily - by throwing money at it.

In our society debt is frequently viewed as shameful This means that its vicitms are often initially unable to come to terms with their situation, and then are faced with a crushing sense of despair as its reality dawns on them. They experience feelings of guilt and shame, mixed with terrible loneliness and isolation. Creditors seem threatening, and it can feel as though there is no one to turn to for help and no escape from the trap they have fallen into. All this is why access to friendship, support and good advice provides such an important lifeline.

Of course, no one ever got out of debt just by having understanding friends. Practical help is also required. Sometimes what is desperately needed is financial investment to help them begin to recover their standing. But the truth is that without detailed and careful advice, even such phil-anthropic action can simply end up as a case of throwing good money after bad. What those in debt often need more than anything else is sound, professional advice on budg-eting skills, dealing with creditors, benefits, savings and investment, together with the friendship and reassurance to see them through.

Project Ideas

• Low

Support the work of existing local or national groups already dealing with debt and poverty, such as Credit Ac-tion. As well as giving advice themselves, Credit Action provide resources to churches and other organisations con-cerned about helping people in debt. Speakers and materi-als are also available. And remember that you might be surprised by how many people within your church strug-gle with budgeting and debt, and how much good can be done by providing help simply within that context - let alone beyond it.

• Medium

Set up a debt advice and counselling centre. This might be run by your church, or by a group of churches working together. You can choose to operate it from as little as one morning or afternoon a week through to providing a full-time service, offering both pastoral and financial counselling. It is obviously vital that all your counsellors or advisors have received professional training. Shortsighted or bad advice will leave your clients in a worse situation than they started with - at the same time as possibly landing your centre in the middle of a law suit! Financial advice, other than in the broadest general terms, is regulated by the Financial Services Act.

• High

Set up a Credit Union. Credit Unions are non-profit making bodies established to provide a savings and loan service for their members. Anyone can be a member, provided they agree to keep to the rules and have something in common with other members. When you join a Credit Union, all your outstanding debts are usually consolidated: ie, paid off at once by the Union, which you then repay at minimal interest over an agreed period of time. After that, members are encouraged to put money into the Credit Union, as savings, and are usually allowed to borrow twice as much as they invest. Credit Unions don't merely help those in debt; they can help people learn how to save and budget as well, enabling them to enjoy things, such as holidays, that they would otherwise never be able to afford.

For further information, contact:

Evangelical Alliance, Whitefield House, 186 Kennington Park Road, London SE11 4BT. Tel: 0171 207 2100

Credit Action, Jubilee Centre, 3 Hooper Street, Cambridge CB1 2NZ. Tel: 01223 324034

Association of British Credit Unions, Unit 307, Westminster Business Square, 33 Kennington Lane, London SE11 5QY

2. Education

Education is a vital key to prosperity. As Francis Bacon once said, 'Knowledge itself is power.' Throughout history, dictators have attempted to control education as a means of controlling the population. And as we saw in Part One, even small differences in educational funding and resources available to different groups can, over time, produce the kind of 'savage inequalities' that concern educators such as Jonathan Kozol. Although education is not the kind of thing we normally tend to think of when we think of suffering, a quality education can help people cope with other forms of suffering, whilst its lack will compound their problems. The whole area of education is a vivid example of the way in which, for all the good will in the world, people can be discriminated against by something as impersonal as a system.

Education is not just about going to school and passing exams. It's about discovering who you are and how you relate to the world around you. It consists not only of acquiring basic information, but also the ability to analyse and interpret this and all other information. Most importantly of all, a good education will equip the learner to make wise and mature decisions, enabling them more adequately to cope with life and its pressures. So it should enhance their quality of life and relationships and give them a greater element of control over their circumstances and environment, rather than letting them be controlled by them.

Project Ideas

• Low

Become more involved as a church in your local schools. Since many schools are underfunded, you might consider sponsoring a local school, purchasing books or computers, or getting together with the school governors to explore other forms of raising money to pay for vital resources. If someone in the church has a child at the school, encourage them to get more involved by becoming a parent-governor. Regularly pray for and support the work of any teachers in your congregation. Explore creative ways to stimulate ongoing interest in their work. On top of this, take a greater interest in the wider issue of education, supporting groups like Care for Education and Scripture Union.

• Medium

Appoint a teacher, regional children's worker or schools team. Teachers are a school's most valuable asset, and in many places they are in short supply. Your church, or group of local churches, could sponsor an additional qualified teacher or pastoral worker for a local school. Alternatively, you could set up a schools project like Drop Zone. Run by Oasis, Drop Zone is concerned with the all-round development of pupils in inner-city London: physical, intellectual, emotional, social, and spiritual. Its schools workers take everything from sports lessons to classes on image, drugs, the media, sex education, ethics, etc. Scripture Union workers cover the same sort of ground, in primary and secondary schools, acting both as schools liaison for a church and as vitally needed support staff for local schools. They are a welcome and valuable asset to many schools in the area they cover.

• High

Set up a nursery school. About one third of all UK schools are church schools, often called 'voluntary schools', funded by both the church and the statutory authorities. Some are indistinguishable from state schools, whilst others have created a more blatantly Christian environment. Now the shortage of nursery school places, admitted by all the major political parties, presents churches with the opportunity to become intimately involved in the first level of education. A nursery school could, once again, be the initiative of one church or a group of local churches. Obviously such an ambitious project requres a significant investment of time and money over an open-ended period, as well as close co-operation with the various statutory authorities. Care for Education or the Evangelical Alliance should be able to put you in touch with other churches working in this field.

For further information, contact:

Evangelical Alliance, Whitefield House, 186 Kennington Park Road, London SE11 4BT. Tel: 0171 207 2100

Scripture Union, 207-209 Queensway, Bletchley, Milton Keynes MK2 2EB. Tel: 01908 856 000

CARE for Education, 53 Romney Street, London SW1P 3RF. Tel: 0171 233 0455.

3. Homelessness

A generation ago, the stereotypical homeless person was an old drop out from society who found comfort in a blanket and a bottle of whisky. Today, there is no stereotype. All sorts of people become homeless for all sorts of reasons: the lack of affordable housing, the reduction in the number of council houses available, the loss of a job, an inability to keep up the rent or mortgage repayments, changes in social security regulations, family breakdown, inadequate resources for children leaving local authority care, inadequate resources for Care in the Community... the list seems endless, but the effect is the same. And those who sleep rough on the street are merely the tip of a much larger iceberg which includes the vast numbers of single people and families living in various kinds of temporary accommodation and squats.

Homelessness is a complex problem with no simple solution. Most homeless people desperately want to move into proper accommodation, but find that getting a job or the money to pay for this kind of housing is extremely difficult without a permanent address in the first place. Some people become homeless because they have never been taught how to budget, or because they are unaware of or naive about the pitfalls of owning or renting property until it's too late. But whatever the reason for their situation, when people become homeless, their self-esteem usually hits rock bottom, adding to their inability to get out of their predicament.

Project Ideas

• Low

Give time and/or money to organisations helping homeless people, such as Shelter, Centrepoint, The Shaftesbury Society, a local housing trust or food and clothing scheme ... or even Oasis! Contact them to find out how you can help. Although it's tempting to give money to individual homeless people, your cash will actually be used far more effectively by groups which tackle the problem of homelessness at a more structural level. You can help either by giving as an individual or by organising a special event / Sunday to highlight the issues involved, creating an opportunity for your audience to give their time or other resources.

• Medium

Set up a rent/deposit scheme. Young, single homeless people and childless couples, who are on low incomes but ineligible for immediate housing by local authorities, often find it very difficult to get suitable and affordable accommodation. Rent/deposit schemes provide support for this type of homeless person. They help them to get (renewable) 6-month tenancies in privately rented accommodation, by providing them with the up-front deposit and a guarantee to the landlord that the rent will be paid in full. They also protect their clients by vetting landlords and properties to make sure that they are offering a fair deal; by helping tenants get whatever state benefits they're entitled to; and by representing the interests of tenants where the landlord is clearly in default of contract. But they provide help for landlords as well by vetting potential tenants to make sure (as far as possible) that they are genuine and suitable, and then by putting good business their way. The Shaftesbury Society is currently involved in setting up a scheme like this in Merton, South London, which it hopes can be replicated elsewhere.

• **High**

Set up a hostel. As part of its work with homeless people, Oasis runs two hostels: No.3 and No.24. Young, single homeless people are referred to No.3 by churches or other organisations, and offered a place in the hostel for one year, if this seems appropriate and there is a place spare. In No.3, they are helped to find work, encouraged to think positively about their future and taught self-sufficiency. After a year, if they still don't feel ready to move into privately-rented accomodation, they have the opportunity of a place in No.24, which takes the process further. The aim is to equip young homeless people with the skills they need to live normal, independent lives in adequate housing. There is obviously a need for many more schemes like this in towns throughout the UK, as well as for similar projects working with other groups of homeless people, such as single parents or young families without the skills and support to cope on their own.

For further information, contact:

Evangelical Alliance, Whitefield House, 186 Kennington Park Road, London SE11 4BT. Tel: 0171 207 2100

Oasis Trust, 87 Blackfriars Rd, London SE1 8HA. Tel: 0171 928 9422

The Shaftesbury Society, 16 Kingston Road, London SW19 1JZ. Tel: 0181 542 5550

4. The Third World

The 'Third World' is an increasingly inaccurate term. Some-times called the 'Two-Thirds World', because it includes two thirds of the world's land and population, or the 'Developing World', because the countries within it are moving toward the development of Western industrial societies, it originally referred to those 'non-aligned' countries which did not count as either part of the First World (developed Western nations) or the Second World (developed Communist Bloc nations)

The term, 'Third World', officially refers to countries, or parts of countries, in which the vast majority of people live close to or below the UN definition of absolute poverty: the bare essentials needed to survive. However, the harsh economic realities of modern life have resulted in strict divisions between rich nations and poor ones meaning less and less. At the end of the 1980s, for instance, standard economic indicators suggested that Brazil was not really a Third World nation, but the condition of its millions of poor people told a very different story.

The people of Third World areas live in a huge poverty trap. They survive either by growing subsistence crops (only what they need for their own food) or cash crops (such as coffee, bananas, sugar, etc) which are then sold for a pittance to companies which process and sell them on. Because these people don't have the money, skills or opportunity to set up their own processing factories or marketing companies, they remain at the mercy of national or multinational companies which make big profits by purchasing raw materials from them very cheaply. Their poverty also often results in their inability to obtain decent housing, education, health-care, sanitation, protection, and political or human rights. And, as I showed in Chapter Four, because they have so little to start with, they are far more vulnerable when natural disasters strike.

Project Ideas

• **Low**

Support the work of charities such Tear Fund, The Jubilee Campaign, World Vision, Christian Aid, Oxfam, Christmas Cracker etc. All of these organisations, and many more, work at both the hand-to-mouth 'Aid' level ('give someone a fish and they have food for a day') and the more structural 'Development' level ('teach someone to fish and they have food for a lifetime'). Raise awareness of Third World issues in your teaching and preaching, and money through special events. You could also sell 'Fairly Traded' goods, such as foods, clothing, jewellery, stationery, gifts, etc. Fairly Traded goods are those where growers or workers have banded together to produce their own product, bypassing the big companies. For instance, Tear Fund produce Fairly Traded tea, and Oxfam has combined with three other charities to produce Café Direct, a Fairly Traded ground or instant coffee available at most supermarkets.

• Medium

Sponsor a particular project or person involved in development work. For instance, your church should think seriously about sponsoring one of its own members to work overseas in a Third World environment, offering their skills to help people trapped in poverty improve their living conditions. Or your youth group could get involved in Christmas Cracker, running one of a variety of short-term projects designed to raise both money and awareness. Since its start in 1989, Christmas Cracker has raised over £4 million through the efforts of young people throughout the UK running 'Eat Less, Pay More' restaurants, 'Tune in, Pay Out' radio stations, Fairly Traded 'Really Useful Present Stores', and 'Cracker' local newspapers.

• High

Set up and help run a housing project, employment initiative, health-care centre, sanitation project, school, or even church building in a Third World country. A growing number of churches are becoming involved in this kind of partnership project. The personal nature of the link between a Western church and a Third World community means that both benefit by becoming involved with each other, truly making the project one of partnership rather than charity. Such initiatives should not be entered into without careful consideration - there are a great many organisational, cultural and bureaucratic pitfalls to avoid.

That's why it makes so much sense to work with the support and backing of an umbrella organisation with a good track record, such as Tear Fund.

For further information, contact:

Evangelical Alliance, Whitefield House, 186 Kennington Park Road, London SE11 4BT. Tel: 0171 207 2100

Christmas Cracker, Cornerstone House, 5 Ethel Street, Birmingham B2 4BE. Tel: 0121 633 0873

Tear Fund, 100 Church Road, Teddington, Middlesex TW11 8QE. Tel: 0181 977 9144

111

Appendix

A Specimen Community Questionnaire

WARNING: The following Community Questionnaire is nothing more than a specimen: a guide designed to help you devise the right tool for surveying your community. Do not attempt to use it in its present form. Its purpose is solely to give you ideas about format, layout, and the kind of information you might want to gather.

With nearly thirty questions, for instance, it's much too long for you to use as it stands. Your task is carefully to think through exactly what information you really want, and then limit your questions to those areas. It's vital to get the difficult balance right, between gathering enough information on the one hand, and not imposing on people's time and patience on the other. So, having read through this specimen and the guidelines for preparing a community survey in Chapter Seven, you and the rest of your core project team should start work on putting together a questionnaire appropriate for use in your local area.

St Ethelred The Unready Parish Church

Community Survey

THANK YOU for agreeing to be one of the 200 people taking part in our community survey. Its purpose is to enable St Ethelred-the-Unready Parish Church to understand and respond to the needs of the local community.

The survey is arranged in 6 parts, A-F, and will take about 6 minutes to complete. You may choose more than one answer to each question if this seems appropriate. Your answers are anonymous and will only be seen by authorised members of the survey team.

Results of the finished survey will be published in The Middle Wallop Gazette on Friday February 30th.

Community Survey Questionnaire

Date: ....

Section A

1: Are you ❑ Male ❑ Female?

2: Do you consider yourself to be
    ❑ White   ❑ Black   ❑ African   ❑ Asian   ❑ East Asian
    Other: ....

3: How old are you?

    ❑ Under 18 ❑ 18-25 ❑ 26-45 ❑ 46-65 ❑ Over 65

4: How long have you lived in the area?

    ❑ Less than 1 yr ❑ 1-3 years ❑ 3-5 years ❑ 5-10 yrs

    ❑ 10-20 yrs ❑ More than 20 yrs ❑ My entire life

Section B

5: What type of work do you do, if any?

❏ Unemployed ❏ Full-time work
❏ Part-time work ❏ Retired
❏ Full-time education ❏ Part-time education
❏ Homemaker

❏ Self-employed: ....

❏ Industry: ....

❏ Service: ....

❏ Financial: ....

❏ Professional: ....

❏ Other: ....

6: Roughly how much do you earn per week, after tax?

❏ Under £100 (£400 per month)

❏ £100 - £200 (£400 - £800 per month)

❏ £200 - £500 (£800 - £2,000 per month)

❏ Over £500 (£2,000 per month)

7: Do you receive any form of income-related state benefit?

❏ No

❏ Yes: ....

8: Are you

❏ single ❏ married

❏ living with someone

❏ divorced/separated ❏ widowed?

9: Do you have any children?

❑ No [Please go to question 11]

❑ Yes: ..... boys ..... girls

10: What age are your children?

❑ 0-3 yrs ❑ 3-5 yrs ❑ 6-10 yrs

❑ 11-15 yrs ❑ 16-18 yrs ❑ adult

11: Who do you live with?

❑ Partner ❑ Children ❑ Partner & children

❑ Parents ❑ Flatmate(s) ❑ Alone

12: What type of accommodation do you live in?

❑ Hostel ❑ Tower block flat ❑ House flat

❑ Terraced house ❑ Semi-detached house

❑ Detached house

13: Is your accommodation

❏ Tied to your job ❏ Rented from the council

❏ Privately rented ❏ Owned by you?

14: What educational/professional qualifications do you have, if any?

❏ GCSEs (❏ Under 5 ❏ 5-10 ❏ More)

❏ 'A' levels (❏ 1 ❏ 2 ❏ 3 ❏ More)

❏ City & Guilds ❏ NVQ/GNVQ

❏ Diploma ❏ Certificate: ....

❏ Degree ❏ Postgraduate degree

❏ Other: ....

15: Are you, or have you ever been, involved in adult education?
❏ Yes ❏ No

16: What mode of transport do you own, if any?

❑ Car (❑ 1 ❑ 2 ❑ More)

❑ Motorbike

❑ Other: ....

17: How often do you use public transport?

❑ Never ❑ Rarely ❑ Every week ❑ Every day

Section C

18: Would you say that the community has a good cross-section in terms of age?

❑ Yes ❑ No

❑ Comments: ....

19: Would you say that the community has a good cross-section in terms of race?

❑ Yes ❑ No

❑ Comments: ....

20: How would you rate the community as a place to live?

❑ Very good ❑ Good ❑ Average

❑ Poor ❑ Very poor

21: How would you rate the community as a place to bring up children?

❑ Very good ❑ Good ❑ Average

❑ Poor ❑ Very poor

22: How would you rate the involvement of the church (all demoninations) in the local community?

❑ Very high ❑ High ❑ Low ❑ Unnoticeable

Section D

23: In your opinion, what problems does the community face?

❏ Crime

❏ Homelessness

❏ Youth crime

❏ Substandard housing

❏ Violence

❏ Alcoholism

❏ Drugs

❏ Racism

❏ Prostitution

❏ Poverty

❏ Discrimination against disabled people

❏ Discrimination against women

❏ Inadequate eductional facilities

❏ Inadequate medical facilities

❏ Single parenthood

❏ Divorce

❏ Debt

❏ Illness

❏ Unemployment

❏ Loneliness

❏ Lack of facilities for children/young people

❏ Despair

122

24: Which three of these (or other) areas would you say were the most critical?

1: ....

2: ....

3: ....

Section E

25: Would you know where to get help with the following problems?

❏ Drugs

❏ Depression

❏ Alcoholism

❏ Debt

❏ Victim of a crime

❏ Divorce/separation

❏ Domestic violence

❏ Family planning

❏ Sexual harassment

❏ Terminal illness

❏ Racial abuse

❏ Accommodation

❏ Discrimination in work/ housing, etc

❏ Redundancy/unemployment

❏ The death of a relative/ friend

Section F

26: What improvements would you like to see happen in the community?

....

....

....

....

....

27: Who do you think should mainly be responsible for carrying out these improvements?

❑ Individuals   ❑ Local organisations

❑ Charities   ❑ Churches

❑ Local council   ❑ National government

28: In your opinion, what sort of thing should the church be doing in the community?

....

....

....

....

....

Thank you very much for taking the time to complete this Community Survey.